Harry Potter and the Meaning of Life

Engaging with Spirituality
in Christian Mission

Philip Plyming

Curate, Christ Church, Chineham

GROVE BOOKS LIMITED
RIDLEY HALL RD CAMBRIDGE CB3 9HU

Contents

Acknowledgements

I would like to thank the Revd Dr David Wilkinson at the Centre for Christian Communication, St John's College, Durham, for first encouraging me to write on this topic and giving me opportunities to share these thoughts with others. I would also like to thank the Revd Dr Richard Turnbull and the people of Christ Church, Chineham for their support over the first few months of my ministry with them and for giving me the time to complete the manuscript. Thanks also go to the Revd Dr James Saunders, the Revd Mark Saunders and the Revd Dr Ian Paul for their incisive comments on a draft copy of this text. Finally I thank my wife, Dr Annabelle Plyming, for her helpful proof reading, continuing love and support—and letting me read Harry Potter first.

The Cover Illustration is by Peter Ashton

First Impression November 2001
ISSN 0262-799X
ISBN 1 85174 482 7

1

Why Read Harry Potter?

When the Christmas edition of *Radio Times* features a radio programme on its front cover, you know something remarkable is going on. Radio 4 FM had cleared its Boxing Day 2000 schedule for over eight hours of uninterrupted Harry Potter, read by Stephen Fry, and thus a young wizard was the Christmas face of *Radio Times*. Many Christmas traditions came to a stop on that Boxing Day as families sat glued to their radios.

This was just one example of the incredible phenomenon that is Harry Potter. The film version has released another whirl of Harry Potter mania in schools and in the papers all over the world. There are several key features of this phenomenon.

First, the sales. When *Harry Potter and the Philosopher's Stone* came out in 1997 it sold 150,000 copies in the first few months, an incredible feat for a first-time unknown author. When *Harry Potter and the Goblet of Fire* came out in summer 2000, there was an initial print run in this country alone of 1.5 million copies. These figures showed that something special was going on.

Second, the author. J K Rowling's rags-to-riches story has been regularly reprised by the newspapers: single mother, living off welfare, writing in cafés in Edinburgh, not enough money to heat the flat...[1] The truth is probably somewhat less dramatic, as Rowling herself has often sought to make clear; her time living off state benefit was not as long as some claim. Whatever the case, Rowling is now one of the richest women in the country, and the story of a single mother having such success has seemed to capture the public imagination. J K Rowling is hot property.

Third, the appeal. Harry Potter's appeal stretches across the world and across the age gap. The books have found success wherever they have been translated—so far 66 million copies in 200 languages. Hence companies fell over themselves to sign up merchandizing deals with the film. When Coca-Cola announced such a deal last year, a spokesman announced '*Both Harry Potter and Coca-Cola reach deep into the heart of local communities around the world to add a little bit of magic to people's everyday lives.*' This corny statement may be a sign of relentless corporate consumerism, but it also shows the worldwide appeal of Harry Potter.

And it is not just children who have fallen in love with Harry Potter. Adults are reading the stories in droves. Bloomsbury has decided to bring

---

1   M Shapiro, *J K Rowling: The Wizard Behind Harry Potter* (London: John Blake, 2000) rehearses this story more extensively than most.

out special adult editions of Harry Potter for grown ups who might be embarrassed to be seen buying or reading a children's book. Parents have been known to start reading Harry Potter to their children as a bedtime story and then finish it themselves that night.

All of the above would be enough reason to look at Harry Potter from a Christian perspective. That Harry Potter is a significant contemporary phenomenon is beyond doubt, and that Christians should engage with contemporary culture is hopefully not a point to be debated.

However, there is another good reason for reading the Harry Potter books —they are genuinely very fine stories. People who have not read them are sometimes suspicious of their success, believing it to be all hype and merchandizing. They believe that the books are formulaic children's stories that have simply been well publicised. But the truth is that all the publicity came second. The initial success of Harry Potter was that children and adults read and enjoyed the stories and told their friends.

Thus the ultimate defining characteristic of the Harry Potter phenomenon is neither the sales nor the author nor the wide appeal, but rather the stories themselves. On one level they are children's tales about a boy's adventures at a school for wizards, told with tension, surprises and humour. There is also something of the detective story in the narratives. But it is generally acknowledged that they go deeper than that. The books handle profound questions and themes that strike at the heart of what it is to be human. Questions of good and evil, the nature of authentic relationships, mortality, wisdom and human choice are all dealt with in ways that are engaging and challenging, and which highlight the paucity of discussion elsewhere. It may thus be justifiably claimed that the books do have an inherent spirituality, and it is for this reason that others who wish to take these existential questions further, including Christians, find them so attractive.

So, why read Harry Potter? Not because others tell you you ought to, or because everyone else is, but because the stories themselves deserve it. They are rich and engaging narratives that touch the reader deeply and stimulate further thought. And, as I found when I first picked up Harry Potter in 1998, they are such ripping yarns that you cannot put them down again!

This booklet is an attempt to engage with the spirituality of Harry Potter for two reasons: first, because as a Christian I want to engage with any text or narrative that asks similar questions to ones I am interested in; second, because in so doing I am engaging with contemporary culture and thereby discovering new ways of sharing the Christian faith relevantly. My conclusions will thus concern Christian faith, contemporary culture and building bridges between the two.

2
Something To Be Scared Of?

Christians and Harry Potter

But should Christians read Harry Potter at all? Is the story of the young wizard appropriate for Christian children (or adults, for that matter)? Much media exposure has been given to Christians (mostly in the US) who have had Harry Potter banned from schools or taken their children out of English lessons where the books are being read. Worried Christian parents in Britain have spoken to me about their concern that their child might be influenced by the occult. Christians have protested outside Gloucester Cathedral where part of the new Harry Potter movie was filmed. On the other hand there have been Christians who have been keen to 'baptize' Harry Potter, seeing the stories as wholly compatible with Christian faith. Services have taken place around a Harry Potter theme, with the vicar robed as Albus Dumbledore umpiring a game of Quidditch in the pews.[2] Where should Christians stand?

The chief area of concern among Christians is that the stories, with their mention of wizards and witches, spells and charms, encourage children to dabble in the occult. This argument has been rehearsed most extensively by Richard Abanes in *Harry Potter and the Bible*.[3] His working assumption is that the books are soaked with references to the occult which encourage young readers to assume that it is normal and harmless. He traces in some detail the way Rowling has drawn on past and present magical activities in her naming of episodes and characters in the stories. For example, he highlights how Nicolas Flamel, the 'philosopher' in *Harry Potter and the Philosopher's Stone*, really did exist; he was a French alchemist in the 1300s who was said to have discovered the secret of eternal life.[4] Abanes uses this and other discoveries to argue that the books have a sub-text of introducing young people to occult tradition and practice. Other Christians take up his point in less detail and argue that children's minds will be corrupted by reading stories which include spells and curses and which are thus clearly incompatible with a Christian faith that has no place for magic and occult forces. This concern is raised by John Houghton in *A Closer Look at Harry Potter*.[5]

It is also worth mentioning briefly two other concerns of Abanes. First, he argues that the books are too frightening for young children as they include

2   See an article in *Reader* magazine (July 2001) by Mike Truman, Reader at All Saints,' Guildford.
3   R Abanes, *Harry Potter and the Bible: The Menace behind the Magick* (Camp Hill, Pennsylvania: Horizon Books, 2001).
4   Abanes, *Harry Potter and the Bible*, pp 26-27.
5   J Houghton, *A Closer Look at Harry Potter* (Eastbourne: Kingsway, 2001).

scenes of violence and darkness.[6] Second, he maintains that the books are unhelpful for Christian children because they seem to endorse a moral approach to life that is incompatible with Christian ethics. Highlighting largely cases of 'bad language' and misdemeanours which go unpunished, Abanes says that what he calls 'Potterethics' renders the Harry Potter stories inappropriate for Christians to read.[7]

There is not space here to examine each of the above arguments in detail; however, a couple of preliminary points may be made. First, the stories are actually much less about wizards and spells than an initial glance at the synopsis might indicate. Indeed, they are not really 'about' wizards or the occult at all, but rather about characters in a quasi-fantasy world where magical things happen. When I ask children what Harry Potter is about, the answers revolve more around what he gets up to at school with his friends, and how he struggles against Voldemort, than the fact that he is a wizard who can perform various spells. Indeed, on one level the stories are about Harry and his friends, in most senses completely normal children; on another level, as I will argue later, they are an exploration of deep existential themes. They are only an advert for the occult if one reads them in a literalistic way which only boring adults seem to do. Yes, they do include words which traditionally make Christians jumpy, but children know they are stories and read them as such.[8]

Second, we must listen to J K Rowling's repeated assertions that in writing the Harry Potter books she was not seeking to make the occult attractive. She has stated that she does not believe in magic in the way it is presented in the books. There has been no evidence produced that Rowling has any connection to the world of the occult others accuse her of advertising. It would seem wise to treat the internet rumours concerning Rowling with a healthy scepticism.

Third, it should be clear that these books are not suitable for young children, but neither are many other highlights of children's literature, for example *Lord of the Rings* or *Lord of the Flies*. But just because some of the scenes are too scary for most 6-year-olds does not mean that they are unsuitable for most 10-year-olds.

Richard Abanes has produced a very thorough text and clearly has a detailed knowledge of the occult practices and publications. He is thus able to show that there is common ground between historical and contemporary

---

6   See for example *Harry Potter and the Bible*, pp 39-42.
7   *ibid*, pp 67-71.
8   See A Goddard 'Harry Potter and the Quest for Virtue' and M Masson 'The Harry Potter Debate' in *Anvil*, Vol 18, No 3. These are both stimulating articles which argue that Harry Potter is more an alternative imaginative universe with a different technology than an advert for the world of the occult.

magical customs and those described in Harry Potter. However, because he seems unable to go beyond a literalistic reading of Harry Potter and engage with wider questions as to how the books work as stories, he fails to show convincingly why this common ground matters. His conclusions are considerably weakened as a result and one is left with the firm belief that in general, if Christians were a bit more prepared to read Harry Potter with the imagination that as a story it deserves and not as a tract, they would be less worried about the effect the book might have on children.

Does all this mean, then, that we need not be scared of Harry Potter? Yes, it does. The texts are not the occult propaganda some Christians assume them to be, and the threat to older children's minds is not great because they can actually realize they are reading a story not a documentary.

This does not mean that Christians can relax completely, unconcerned by any aspect of the Harry Potter phenomenon. The film and associated merchandizing may well play the wizard theme more strongly than the stories do. Also, the flurry of books which are seriously promoting wizardry, and which are flying on Harry Potters's commercial coattails, may fan the flames of an existing interest in the occult, and this should concern us, together with other destructive influences on children. We need to be alive to all potential harmful influences and pray accordingly. But our conclusion must be that the Harry Potter books themselves are not the threat to children's souls that some Christians maintain.

Engaging Harry Potter Responsibly

Indeed, the most important way to respond to Harry Potter is not to put our own or our children's heads in the sand, but rather to help them and us engage creatively and responsibly with the stories as they are. My advice to Christian parents would be to read the stories with your children and then talk with them about what they thought of them. The premise of this booklet is that there is much spiritual material to discuss so it should be a helpful starting point.

But the question remains: if, as I argued in chapter 1, the books do have an inherent spirituality, how do we Christians engage with it responsibly? Let me outline how we should *not* do it before suggesting an approach which will form the heart of this study.

What we should *not* do is go to Harry Potter with a certain set of Christian questions or expect to find there analogies to the Christian faith which we can use in sermons or talks. This may seem a surprising thing to say. Surely we go into the world seeking Christ where we can find him, and seeking to make connections with the Christian faith wherever we come across them? This is all true, but if we make this the first step in our reading of Harry Potter we betray a somewhat arrogant belief that all stories and texts are in essence Christian as long as we look hard enough, and abuse a text which, unlike the *Narnia* chronicles and *Lord of the Rings*, makes no claim to be written from a Christian standpoint.

Thus to argue that there are certain questions which can be asked of any story, including 'does anyone in this story play a Christ-like role?' is to encourage cherry picking the Christian bits out of a story without necessarily engaging with the narrative on a deeper level. Similarly, it seems to me wholly disingenuous for Christians to take away from Harry Potter that Dumbledore is like Aslan and thus like Jesus and Hogwarts is like the safety of heaven. Christians may well find themselves being reminded of things like this when they are the reading the books, but that does not mean in so doing they are saying anything helpful about the spirituality of the Harry Potter series. In fact, they are probably flattening out both Harry Potter and their own faith.

Indeed, the problem of this approach is that it shows Christians wanting to read the books on their own terms, wanting to find answers that will accord with their own faith. 'How does this reflect back on my own faith?' may well be a comfortable question for Christians to ask, but it should not be the first question we set ourselves when we read a book. The first question should be 'what is this book about?' And it is a question which should not be answered too quickly, because books are often 'about' more than we think they are.

If we do not answer the question 'what is this book about?' carefully and honestly, then two things will happen. First, we will show ourselves to be poor readers and listeners of other stories which is not appropriate to the way God is calling us to share the gospel in the world. Paul's missionary strategy in Athens (recorded in Acts 17) involved starting with the culture of the day and then using that as his basis for sharing faith. Second, our conclusions will not carry as much weight because it will be seen that they are based on a hasty and self-serving reading of the text. For effective dialogue and mission to take place we need to avoid both these eventualities and listen carefully to the story first.

So then, if the approach of going to Harry Potter with certain Christian questions or sermon illustrations in mind is not appropriate, what might a more honest reading look like? I have argued that the first question we should ask is 'what are the books about?' I suggest that in order to answer this question we need to do the following. Instead of reading Harry Potter with one foot in the world of Hogwarts and another firmly in the Christian world, we need to start to read Harry Potter with both feet in Hogwarts. That is to say, we must read Harry Potter on its own terms. We must appreciate it for what it is: a children's story enjoyed by adults as well, not written with any explicit spiritual purpose in mind, but obviously deep in its reflections and challenges. Having both feet firmly in Hogwarts, we can then try to reflect more thoroughly on what Harry Potter is really about. What are the questions which the stories raise again and again? What are the recurring themes? What seems important in all the four books so far?

The next step is describing those main themes and questions in the way the books themselves deal with them. This is an appreciation of the fundamental themes of the Harry Potter series, and we must avoid here using any Christian language which is inappropriate. It is in essence a preliminary summary of the spirituality of Harry Potter, framed in deliberately non-Christian terms. Obviously it is going to be a personal choice as to what the main themes are, and that personal choice will of course be framed by one's Christian faith, but if we try to remain as objective as possible better results will be achieved.

Having outlined the main themes and questions the stories raise, we can then reflect back in two ways. First, we can look at how these themes and questions resonate in the rest of contemporary culture. Do we see these themes and questions raised elsewhere? Are the answers similar? Second, we can reflect back on our Christian faith. Does the Christian faith ask similar or different questions? Are the answers the same? Does anything here remind me of my experience as a Christian? The answers to all these questions can form the basis for a relevant way of sharing our faith today.

This is the way I intend to read Harry Potter. I will try to outline four key themes which seem to me pivotal to the stories and as I do that I will see how each theme resonates in today's society and with Christian faith. In essence I am asking questions of three different spiritualities: the spirituality of Harry Potter, as I try to perceive it; the spirituality of contemporary culture; and the spirituality of Christian faith. The difference between my approach and the one I outlined earlier is that I do not try to make Harry Potter into a Christian text too early on.

This introduction has been long but necessary. Now to business and Harry himself.

3
Reflecting on Key Themes

1. Transformation of Character

One of the most sparkling features of the Harry Potter books is the characters. They are a wonderfully rich and diverse bunch with a depth of personality and expression that is a joy to encounter. Their names are not the only exciting things about them. They combine authentic human characteristics with splendidly eccentric habits: the giant Hagrid with his love for 'interesting' creatures; the deliciously nasty Dursleys with their odd-shaped necks and spoilt son Dudley; the fiercely keen Hermione Granger (there is one in every class); the Weasley family which is worth a study all on its own; Draco Malfoy, Nearly Headless Nick, the list could go on. These are characters we come to love and relish. They are people we can recognize and whom we can come to know.

Yet I believe the strength of the characterizations in Harry Potter goes beyond this. What I find most interesting in the characters of Harry Potter is that they are subtle, complex and never static. Gone largely are the somewhat two-dimensional characters of Roald Dahl (although the Dursleys do admittedly still fit in this category). In Harry Potter, characters are often defined by not being what they seem. Two examples will make this point— Professor Snape and Sirius Black.

Professor Snape

Professor Snape is introduced as the archetypal cruel and vindictive schoolmaster. He seems to hate Harry, docking housepoints from him at every opportunity and trying to get him expelled. The narrative frequently seems to suggest that it is Professor Snape who is at the bottom of the latest scheme against Harry or Hogwarts. And yet it transpires again and again at the end of the stories that Snape is actually on the side of Hogwarts and thus of Harry. At the end of *The Philosopher's Stone* we discover that it was Professor Snape's spell that was protecting Harry during the Quidditch match; he has saved Harry's life. In *The Goblet of Fire* it becomes clear that while Snape was once a Death Eater in league with Lord Voldemort, he turned against the evil wizard at great personal cost and worked for Dumbledore as a spy. The reader discovers that Snape has actually been very brave. Standing next to Dumbledore at the end, he still has the nasty leer, but there is no doubt that his character is restored. From being the bad egg in the school he is now a key part of the plan to defend it.

Sirius Black

Sirius Black starts with even worse credentials than Professor Snape. In *The Prisoner of Azkaban* he is demonized as a mass-murderer who was conspiring with Voldemort and who betrayed Harry's parents. The reader understands that he has escaped from that darkest of prisons and is out for revenge. The whole school is afraid and when Harry eventually encounters Sirius Black he thinks his end has come. However, the truth is quite the opposite. Sirius Black is not the murderer he was assumed to be. It was not he who betrayed Harry's parents but Peter Pettigrew. Sirius was falsely imprisoned all along. He is in fact Harry's godfather and is restored to that relationship before he has to disappear again. In *The Goblet of Fire*, however, he returns and takes his place alongside Dumbledore with those defending Hogwarts. His restoration is complete.

These are but two examples of characters not being what they seem. Other examples abound: Professor Lupin who is in fact a werewolf; Professor Quirrell who is being inhabited by Voldemort; Gilderoy Lockhart who is an utter fraud as a teacher; Hagrid who in fact has giant blood; Mad-Eye Moody who is not who he seems. There is in many characters a tension between the impression the characters give and the real essence of who they are. A study of the names in Harry Potter reinforces this point. The names often say something about the character, but they are sometimes ironic as the reality of a person is very different. So, while Voldemort and Malfoy give clear hints that they are on the dark side, which is the case, and Lupin really turns out to be a werewolf (*lupus* is the Latin for wolf), Dumbledore is not as bumbling as his name suggests, and Sirius Black is of course anything but dark in his character. Part of the excitement of the narrative is the uncovering of a character's true being, the unveiling of who somebody really is, the restoration of them to their true selves. In Harry Potter there is more going on in people than we imagine, and characters alter and shift in a way that challenges us as readers.

This shift is not always in one direction. But the idea that characters are complicated and can be transformed is an important one across the texts. It is interesting how this is reflected in contemporary culture. Two prevailing views come initially to mind. First is the idea that people are either 100% good or bad. You are either up or you are down—ask Sophie Wessex or Jeffrey Archer. You are on a pedestal and then you are knocked off again. Newspapers divide society into law-abiders and law-breakers and demonize the latter. Second, there seems to be a view that bad people cannot be transformed. 'Lock 'em up and throw away the key' is a popular view we hear. There is no possibility of restoration for Jonathan Aitken, no way back for the killers of James Bulger, no new start possible for sex offenders.

In this context I think that Christian spirituality would find itself more in agreement with Harry Potter than with some of the prevailing views in contemporary culture. Christian faith acknowledges that as human beings we are not all we seem. We are complicated beings, neither perfect nor totally evil. We are made in the image of God (Gen 1.27) and yet we are sinners (Rom 3.23). We have the potential to do great good and yet so often we fail to do it. The apostle Paul knew this tension to be true of humankind generally and in his own life (Rom 7.14–25). God knows that we are complicated people and yet he sees through this to who we could be in him. The encounter Jesus had with the Samaritan woman in John 4 testifies to this work of God. Dumbledore did this with Snape and Sirius Black. God can do this with each one of us.

Repentance and Renewal

More than this, Christians proclaim a gospel of transformation. We cannot agree with a view of human beings that is ultimately static. We want to affirm that God calls his people to be renewed and through the saving work of Christ and empowering of the Holy Spirit enables this to take place. In 2 Cor 5.11–21 Paul is clear that God is about making 'new creations,' forming changed people, reconciled to God through Christ. The Christian God does not lock up bad people and throw away the key; God is always showing the way back, through repentance and faith. The ministry of Jesus included offering life to those whom others thought incapable of change—adulterers (John 4.1–42), tax collectors (Mark 2.13–17), prostitutes (Luke 7.36–50), lepers (Matthew 8.1–4). He is able to restore anybody to life in all its fullness, as forgiven, chosen, loved people.[9] The stories of the changed lives in Harry Potter—Snape and Sirius Black—are imperfect examples of this truth (are they really transformed, or is it simply our perception that is transformed?), but they are welcome voices in a world hostile to the possibility of restoration. The question remains, however, will there be a new beginning for the Dursleys, or any of the Muggles (non-wizards) for that matter? Christians claim transformation is possible for everyone in Christ (John 3.16; see also the guest list for the Great Banquet in Luke 14.15–24). Whatever the case, this is a part of the spirituality of Harry Potter that we will want to welcome and use to share our own faith.

---

9   Compare Joel 2.25 'I will repay for the years that the swarming locust has eaten.'

2. Choices

It seems to me that there are two underlying questions which stretch across the Harry Potter books. First, how important is fate? There seem to be many people who believe in fate, that things are already decided for us according to a great plan. Some believe that Harry is destined for greatness. Professor Trelawny, the Divination teacher, takes this underlying belief to a wonderful extreme, believing that everything runs according to the stars and the tea leaves. Her phoney predictions not only annoy Hermione but are some of the most humorous parts of *The Prisoner of Azkaban*. The second question is, how important is my blood? That is to say, does it matter what I was born? Certain characters like the Malfoy family and Tom Riddle seem to think it matters a lot. They detest Muggles and Mudbloods (wizards of Muggle parents), and it is around this question that *The Chamber of Secrets* really revolves.

It is against the background of these two questions that the story of the Sorting Hat acquires great significance. The narrative alerts us to its importance as the episode is alluded to more than once.

To recap briefly: it is Harry's first day at Hogwarts. He is taken into the large hall where new pupils are putting on the Sorting Hat and waiting to hear which boarding house the Sorting Hat is going to put them in. Various pupils have had houses allotted to them, and now it is Harry's turn...

> The last thing Harry saw before the hat dropped over his eyes was the hall full of people craning to get a good look at him. Next second he was looking at the black inside of the hat. He waited.
>
> 'Hmm,' said a small voice in his ear. 'Difficult. Very difficult. Plenty of courage, I see. Not a bad mind, either. There's talent, oh my goodness, yes—and a nice thirst to prove yourself, now that's interesting...So where shall I put you?'
>
> Harry gripped the edges of the stool and thought, 'Not Slytherin, not Slytherin'
>
> 'Not Slytherin, eh?' said the small voice 'Are you sure? You could be great, you know, it's all here in your head and Slytherin will help you on the way to greatness, no doubt about that—no? Well, if you're sure— better be GRYFFINDOR'[10]

And so Harry starts an eventful time in Gryffindor house, and avoids Slytherin house which Lord Voldemort was in and which has always had a dubious reputation for producing wizards inclined to the dark side. However, later in *The Chamber of Secrets* Harry realizes that he has some abilities which would make him a natural candidate for Slytherin house. He can speak

10   J K Rowling, *Harry Potter and the Philosopher's Stone* (London: Bloomsbury, 1997) pp 90-91.

Parseltongue (the language of snakes), as could the evil Lord Voldemort, and he seems to have some of his gifts. He becomes desperately unsure of himself and so speaks to Dumbledore, the headmaster.

'So I should be in Slytherin,' Harry said, looking desperately into Dumbledore's face. 'The Sorting Hat could see Slytherin's power in me, and it—'

'Put you in Gryffindor' said Dumbledore calmly. 'Listen to me, Harry. You happen to have many qualities Salazar Slytherin prized in his hand-picked students. His own very rare gift, Parseltongue… resourcefulness… determination…a certain disregard for rules,' he added, his moustache quivering again. 'Yet the Sorting Hat placed you in Gryffindor. You know why that was. Think.'

'It only put me in Gryffindor,' said Harry in a defeated voice, 'because I asked not to go in Slytherin…'

'Exactly,' said Dumbledore, beaming at him once more. 'Which makes you very different from Tom Riddle. It is our choices, Harry, that show what we truly are, far more than our abilities.'[11]

That last sentence has rightly been recognized as one of the most crucial throughout the stories. Dumbledore recasts a similar sentiment when at the end of *The Goblet of Fire* he tells the dithering Cornelius Fudge 'you fail to recognize that it matters not what someone is born, but what they grow to be.'[12]

Thus again and again it is making choices which strikes at the heart of what it means to be human in Harry Potter, not how you were born, what you can do or what others tell you. A belief in fate is shown to be flawed; an emphasis on your family pedigree is undermined by such nasty pieces of work as Draco Malfoy. Harry has to learn that he does not have to listen to others but face up to his responsibility to make choices that will affect his present and shape his future.

This emphasis of choice over and against fate, peer pressure and family pedigree seems to me at the heart of the spirituality in Harry Potter. It also resonates in an interesting way with society today. Despite the undoubted power that consumer choice brings, choice is undermined in many ways. Advertisements on TV tell you that you have to have the latest gadget of fashion to be worth anything at all. The glossy magazines imply that only those with perfect skin have any beauty. Horoscopes say that your fate lies in the stars, so just sit back and enjoy the ride. All of this is effectively saying

11   J K Rowling, *Harry Potter and the Chamber of Secrets* (London: Bloomsbury, 1998) p 245.
12   J K Rowling, *Harry Potter and the Goblet of Fire* (London: Bloomsbury, 2000) p 615.

to people: 'You don't have a choice. This is how it is.'

A similar attitude is sometimes taken to the debate on how we were born. Newspapers seem desperate to put a spin on the latest research from the human genome project to argue we are simply what we are born with, and this affects sexual, criminal and emotional behaviour. There seems little willingness to engage with the tough questions about nature and nurture, and rather a desire to abdicate responsibility. 'I was born like it' is often the refrain; it is a spirituality firmly at odds with that of Harry Potter.

How do both of these resonate with Christian faith? I believe that the sceptical view that Harry Potter takes on the issue of fate and genes is an interesting one for the Christian. We maintain it is God who is Lord of all, not some indeterminate fate located in tea leaves or the stars. The core belief of the OT is that God is the Creator God who has also revealed himself in the giving of the divine name and acting to save the people of Israel (Genesis 1; Exodus 3.13–22). He is not an unknown entity but a revealed and living reality. We also want to claim that as humans we were created as free to choose. Both Adam and Eve make choices and are held responsible for these choices (Gen 3.8–19) and the people of Israel are reminded of the choice they have to make in Deut 30.19 ('choose life'). The teaching of Jesus may be understood as reminding his listeners of the choice they are able and have to make (Lazarus and Dives in Luke 16.19–31), and it was this emphasis on choice and decision that characterized the preaching of the early church (Acts 13.13–52). We are morally responsible people who can make choices and who must answer for them. Although our families and our surroundings are important, we must affirm that we are neither machines programmed by our genes nor slaves who have to follow the master of society and its advertising.

This does not mean that in welcoming what Harry Potter has to say on choices and affirming our God-given ability to choose we agree with those Christian moralists who raise individual responsibility to the highest place in our thinking on human society. The whole notion of vocation, of God's calling us to follow a way of life and adopt certain disciplines, involves the free renunciation of absolute freedom of choice—though it brings a freedom all its own. But we do want to thank Harry Potter for giving us the opportunity to say, in the face of a society which believes otherwise, that humans do not have to be slaves to the voices without or the genes within.

3. *Good and Evil*

With even a cursory reading of the Harry Potter stories it becomes clear that the struggle between good and evil lies at the heart of the Hogwarts story. The stories are set against a backdrop of conflict and battle between good, in the shape of the Potters, Dumbledore and Hogwarts, and evil, in the shape of Lord Voldemort, the Death Eaters and Peter Pettigrew. The novels are full of the language of trials, battles and duels. This general and underlying conflict is brought into focus at the end of each story with a physical confrontation between the forces of evil, usually in the shape of Lord Voldemort, and Harry himself. Harry has escaped death on three occasions already; he is the focus for Voldemort's attack but the battle is broader than a personal vendetta. It is a shadow to all that goes on at Hogwarts. The Defence against the Dark Arts lessons are not simply for academic interest.

There are several interesting aspects of this battle between good and evil. First, the battle is ongoing, that is to say, the conflict between good and evil is not a temporary phenomenon but has a past, a present and a future. The present stories are shaped by a bigger story, namely the time when years ago the wizarding world was taken over by the dark forces, when Voldemort was gaining ascendancy. This episode is alluded to by many characters on different occasions; its coming to end with the death of Harry's parents and Voldemort's defeat by the infant Harry has passed into wizarding folklore, such was its importance.

Harry knows that evil is not a fleeting reality in his world but an ever-present danger. Soon after his defeat of Voldemort at the end of *The Philosopher's Stone*, Harry asks Dumbledore:

'Well, Voldemort's going to try other ways of coming back, isn't he? I mean, he hasn't gone, has he?'

'No Harry, he has not. He is still out there somewhere, perhaps looking for another body to share…not being truly alive, he cannot be killed. He left Quirrell to die; he shows just as little mercy to his followers as his enemies. Nevertheless, Harry, while you may only have delayed his return to power, it will merely take someone else who is prepared to fight what seems a losing battle next time—and if he is delayed again, why, he may never return to power.'[13]

Thus the battle between good and evil is not to be understood as the result of a bit of bad luck but rather as the norm in Harry Potter's world.

The second feature of the battle between good and evil is that both forces have a human face. The Dark Arts are not a cosmic power we cannot see. In

13 *Philosopher's Stone*, p 216.

Voldemort they achieve concrete reality, and in Dumbledore the forces of good achieve the same. The result of this is that the meta-narrative of the struggle between good and evil is not the abstract conflict it could become. Good and evil are not nebulous powers but embodied realities. That they are embodied makes the conflict more personal. It challenges those in the wizarding world to decide who they will follow; the battle is out in the open. The reader understands that to side with Dumbledore is to fight for good; to go with Voldemort is to side with evil.

The third aspect of the struggle is that evil needs to be defeated by good. At this point in the series of books we find ourselves as at the interval of a play. We know what the issues are, but we do not know how they will end. *The Goblet of Fire* sharpened the issue considerably. Voldemort has now returned to embodied life and poses a threat to all. Dumbledore is preparing to close ranks at Hogwarts and fight for survival. We are not certain how it will all end, but the view from the final pages of *The Goblet of Fire* is that evil must be defeated. Nothing less will do.[14]

So it is this battle between good and evil that forms the essence of existence for the characters of the Harry Potter stories. Good has won thus far. We are interested to see whether it will win the final battle.

Harry Potter is not the first series of books—children's or otherwise—to be shaped by a battle between good and evil, but its incredible popularity enables us to reflect critically on a society which is lapping the stories up. Popular media seems comfortable with the language of evil when it is applied in individual cases, but has largely lost the vocabulary of an ongoing battle between good and evil. For example, the word 'evil' is used to describe usually particularly horrible crimes such as the genocide in Rwanda or the murder of Jamie Bulger. But anyone who suggests that there is a continuing struggle between good and evil is accused of adopting an ancient worldview, no longer relevant to today's modern world. Evil is personified in especially bad people; it is not seen an omnipresent force.

This is why it is especially interesting that the Harry Potter books are so popular, when their spirituality so patently includes a battle between good and evil. Is this a grudging acceptance because in all other respects the books are so entertaining? Or are people happy to read about a conflict which they know deep down is still going on?

Christians will certainly hope the latter is true. Indeed, this is another area where there is, or perhaps where there should be, a good deal of correlation between the spirituality of Harry Potter and Christian spirituality. Two reflections spring immediately to mind. First, Christians will want to affirm that there is a battle going on out there between good and evil. Ephesians

---

14 The death of Cedric Diggory in *Goblet of Fire* highlights the urgency of defeating Voldemort.

6.12 is a key text but there are other references as well (John 16.11; Col 1.16; 2.15). The Church of England new baptism service in Common Worship, although seeking to avoid language that is seen as too triumphalistic, still includes the prayer which begins 'Fight valiantly as a disciple of Christ against sin, the world and the devil.' Christians should believe that the battle is being fought day by day in individuals, in communities and in structures. It is true that this battle has been reduced by some Christians into a privatized struggle for our souls, but the evidence for a struggle going on in all parts of our world is very strong. Evil is not simply an issue for those who have committed really heinous crimes; rather it is an issue for all of us as we each make our own decisions where we stand in the battle. Say this normally, and you would probably be laughed at; say you are saying this having reflected on the Harry Potter stories, you will probably get a more sympathetic audience. Indeed, as Christians we would do well to reflect on whether our understanding of the battle between good and evil is really broad enough.[15]

Secondly, Christians will be able to maintain that evil has already been defeated. Book 7 is probably a good three years off, and so we do not yet know how it will end. Christians claim to know the end of the real story. We believe in Christ's death and resurrection; we see the victory of God over evil (1 John 5.4); we see sin and death defeated (1 Cor 15.54–57). Obviously we still live in a fallen world where evil continues to hold sway, but the final battle has taken place. We are living in the in-between times, waiting for the victory to be complete (Rom 16.20). Christian spirituality should not be triumphalistic, but it is based on a firm belief that God has triumphed and thus we can claim the defeat of evil in our own lives.

4. Relationships

In a story set in a school it is inevitable that relationships are going to play a large part in the story and thus in the spirituality of the narrative. What characterizes the Harry Potter book is the diverse and interesting nature of these relationships. As far as Harry himself is concerned, they exist on at least two different levels. First, there are the relationships Harry has with the other pupils at school. Harry runs the full gamut of experience in this respect: he is adored and despised by the same people at different times; he knows Ron's support, but also his jealousy; he fancies a girl, Cho; he has an enemy, Draco Malfoy. He has supportive relationships with adults, namely Hagrid and Dumbledore, but also strained relationships, as with Snape. Yet the crucial aspect of all of this is that Harry does not live his life on his own. When no-one, not even Ron, speaks to him because he has been entered into the TriWizard tournament, he just is not himself.

---

15   M Masson, 'The Harry Potter Debate' p 195.

The next few days were some of Harry's worst at Hogwarts. The closest he had ever come to feeling like this had been during those months, in his second year, when a large part of the school had suspected him of attacking his fellow students. But Ron had been on his side then. He thought he could have coped with the rest of the school's behaviour if he could just have had Ron back as a friend, but he wasn't going to try and persuade Ron to talk to him if Ron didn't want to. Nevertheless, it was lonely, with dislike pouring in on him from all sides.[16]

Harry, the Harry who has powers others can only dream of, does not seek to rely on himself, but rather draws on the support of friends. This is no super-hero but a boy to whom relationships are vital if he is truly to be himself.

Absent Friends

Secondly, there are the relationships with those who are physically ab-sent. This is a particularly interesting aspect of the Harry Potter spirituality. In *The Goblet of Fire* Harry has a special relationship with Sirius Black by post and similarly with Dumbledore even when the great man is not there. In-deed, Dumbledore seems to know that physical presence is not necessary for authentic relationship. When that great headmaster is threatened with losing his job and leaving Hogwarts he says *'you will find that I will only truly have left this school when none here are loyal to me.'*[17] Physical presence is only part of a relationship; there are roots which go much deeper.

The prime example of a relationship with someone physically absent is between Harry and his parents who are distant in time as well as space. Harry's parents may well be dead but the relationship he has with them blossoms as throughout his time at Hogwarts he learns more about them. Hagrid gives him some photographs of his parents. Sirius Black tells Harry about the things he and Harry's father, James, used to get up to. Harry learns about how his parents died. He hears the moments of his parents' death at the hands of Voldemort more than once, usually at crucial times, such as when he is fighting Lord Voldemort in *The Goblet of Fire*. He hears his fa-ther's protection of Harry and his mother and he hears his mother sacrific-ing herself for him. Both of these events and the continual reliving of them shape and change Harry's present existence. His relationship with his par-ents, though they are dead, continues to grow and strengthen him for daily living as well as in those particularly dark moments. So, from the end of *The Philosopher's Stone*, when Harry asks Dumbledore why he was not killed, the great man replies:

---

16 *Goblet of Fire*, p 259.
17 *Chamber of Secrets*, p 195.

'Your mother died to save you. If there is one thing Voldemort cannot understand, it is love. He didn't realize that love as powerful as your mother's for you leaves its own mark. Not a scar, no visible sign…to have been loved so deeply, even though the person who loved us is gone, will give us some protection forever.'[18]

This revisiting by Harry of his parents' loving relationship with him gives him strength even though they are now absent. The power of relationships to change a present reality here receives eloquent testimony. It is my hunch that it will receive more in the books to come.

But how does this relationship-shaped spirituality resonate with the spiritualities of popular culture and Christian faith? In a sense our society is entirely comfortable with the language of relationship. The front pages of the broadsheets, as well as the tabloids, are full of news about who is going out with whom, or the latest celebrity divorce. Adverts are dominated by couples either in or seeking a relationship, asking for coffee, driving a new car, enjoying that cut-price holiday. Soaps rely on powerful relationships to drive ratings.

Relationships and Commodities

But there is another side to relationships in contemporary culture as well. In much contemporary media relationships are often talked of as simply another commodity that is added to the portfolio of possessions we individuals carry around. Relationships are something to be acquired and discarded when appropriate. A couple celebrating 50 years of marriage is not news; a spectacular divorce is. This is the world where pre-nuptial agreements are a sign of success (even if they are often ridiculed), where relationships can be abandoned if the benefits are good enough. Dianne Thompson, the head of Camelot, and Veuve Clicquot Business Woman of the Year 2000, is not untypical in saying that she had to sacrifice her marriage for her career, but that it has been worth it. We would probably want to argue that this view of relationships is restricted to a relatively small celebrity and media bubble, but it is influencing all our mindsets, and thus we need to critique it.

The Christian faith has a very different spirituality of relationships, and once again it finds itself in some agreement with the spirituality of Harry Potter. Christian spirituality places relationships at the heart of what it is to be human. Just as we believe in a God who has reached out in a loving relationship with the world he has created, so we believe that human beings are at our most human, our most authentic, in relationships of love and care, supremely with our maker. The prologue of John's gospel is a wonderful

---

18 *Philosopher's Stone*, p 216.

example of this priority of relationships within the plan of God for his world. We see the intimate relationship of the Father God to the Son/Word in vv 1–4, and then the potential relationship as children of God offered to those who will receive Jesus (vv 12–13). We believe that our lives consist neither in the abundance of possessions (Luke 12.15), nor in exclusive self-reliance (Proverbs 3.5–6) and relationships are not to be discarded lightly.

Christian spirituality also knows that relationships do not have to be with someone physically present to be powerful and transforming, for we claim this to be true of our relationship with Jesus. Reading the stories of Harry's parents' death and its continued influence on Harry's life one cannot help but find a strong resonance with the claims Christians make about Jesus. His sacrificial death in our place showed his love for us (1 John 4.10), and the outworking of that death changes our past, our present and our future. It even leaves us with a mark (Rev 7.3–4)! The cross is of course much more than an expression of love, and we believe that through the Holy Spirit Jesus is not absent today, but the truth that a past expression of love can radically alter our present is a key part of how we want to share faith today.

Relationships matter, and past demonstrations of love can change the present. This is at the heart of the spirituality of Harry Potter; it is also a crucial part of the Christian faith which shapes and drives our mission today.

4
Conclusion

We have looked at reasons for reading Harry Potter as a text which befits further study, which clearly raises deep questions surrounding living today, and as a popular contemporary phenomenon with which Christians should want to engage. I hope I have established that although the Harry Potter books do include words which make Christians wary, they are not the occult propaganda some assume them to be, being about much more than wizards and magic. I have suggested a way to read the texts with integrity, highlighting key themes before suggesting correlations or otherwise with the Christian faith. Finally, I identified four key themes from the stories and showed how these reflected in contemporary culture and Christian faith. We can conclude that Harry Potter does have significant areas of agreement with traditional Christian spirituality, and these may be used to encourage dialogue which is a crucial part of mission today.

It is also my hope that I have modelled a way of engaging with contemporary spirituality as part of our mission to share Jesus. By not making J K Rowling into a Christian writer (if she did but know it) or pretending that she is a modern-day Lewis or Tolkein writing out of a Christian world-view, we are showing that it is both possible and important to value the writer and the story on their own terms before tracing implications for our understanding of Christian faith. All readers must feel able to appreciate a story for itself before establishing areas of dialogue with Christian faith. Also, by noting the areas of difference and dissonance between Harry Potter and Christian faith we have shown that it is possible to disagree with a text and still find it very rewarding to study. There is a tendency either so to present the Christian faith that it becomes indistinguishable from the spirituality of Harry Potter or to say that there is no common ground between the two. By listening carefully to the story first and only then considering Christian faith it is possible to reach safer and more enriching conclusions.

What are the wider implications of the approach I suggest? First, by considering Harry Potter as a very significant contemporary phenomenon and seeking to understand and value it on its own terms, we communicate that culture is important. We are not sneering at the books because they are popular, as some Christian academics (and vicars) tend to do, but wanting to join others in reading, enjoying and reflecting on them. We are saying that culture matters. The message of the Incarnation is that God comes and gets involved in the world he made—he starts by calling us from where we are. Because our culture is a key component of where we are, it matters to God. It may not be what God is calling us to, but that does not mean we should ignore it because God certainly does not. By spending time looking at Harry Potter, the Top 10, Eastenders or whatever story grabs us we show that we want to take seriously where people are.

Secondly, by tracing how Christian faith interacts with the questions raised by Harry Potter we communicate that Christian faith is relevant to our world today. So often we claim that Christianity has the answers to our questions, but the questions are not what people outside the church are asking. As we try and discover the questions that Harry Potter, Coronation Street or the latest number one asks of us, and suggest answers that the Christian faith can give, we can justifiably claim that Christianity really is relevant to where people are. Christians believe that their faith is relevant in all ages and situations. By showing that it matches and deals with some of the chief concerns of these key contemporary stories we are demonstrating this to be the case.

Thirdly, by using Harry Potter as a way of considering key elements of the Christian faith, we communicate that a secular story can be used to introduce the story of God, the love of God for us in the life, death and resurrection of our Lord Jesus Christ. It is possible to identify the spirituality of a story by tracing its major themes, and to do so without wishing to make too hasty comparisons with the Christian faith. And this spirituality can then be used as a mirror to the spirituality of our contemporary society and our own Christian faith. It will ask questions of our Christian faith and may lead to prolonged reflection on our own part. But we can be confident that our Christian spirituality will be relevant to the stories of this world, as it testifies to a God who meets every need and can inhabit every story.

Fear Not!

So the conclusion of this booklet is that we need not be afraid. We need not be afraid of Harry Potter, because we have seen that the stories can help us share our faith in a God who transforms complex human lives, who dignifies us to behave as free human beings, who has dealt and is dealing with evil in the world, and who reaches out to us in a loving and self-giving relationship. Harry Potter is not a Christian story, and its message should never be described as Christian, but it has helped us in our reflection on how we can share our Christian faith in relevant ways to a society we want to understand. We can draw on the spirituality of Harry Potter in talks, in schools, in sermons and in conversations with people who share our enjoyment of the books. We can show our appreciation of the stories and share how they reflect on our own lives. This is contemporary apologetics at its best.

And we need not be afraid of other stories either. Some may have a spirituality with which we are more comfortable than others, but we can be confident that almost all can be used to make us reflect creatively on our own faith and our mission to share that with others. However, we must be careful that we do not abuse stories, using them in mission before we have tried to understand them properly, which only leads to inaccurate and unpersuasive conclusions. The first step of engaging with other spiritualities is careful reading and listening.

Harry Potter is only set to get bigger, with more films being planned as well as books. Some parts of the phenomenon may be unattractive; the blatant merchandizing and glamorizing of spells in the film may well be distasteful. However, if Christians can go beyond that they will find in the Harry Potter stories a rich resource not only for reflecting on their own spirituality but also for sharing that with others. There is no need to 'baptize' the Harry Potter stories as Christian to find them useful and rewarding in our mission to share God's love to a needy world. With Harry Potter, and any contemporary spirituality with which we wish to engage, we can discover a spirituality on which we can draw in ways that are fair and honest both to understand better this society which God loves and to share our faith today in that greatest story ever told.

Bibliography

Richard Abanes, *Harry Potter and the Bible: The Menace behind the Magick* (Camp Hill, Pennsylvania: Horizon Books, 2001). A very thorough but rather disturbing book that seeks to highlight the common ground between the world of Harry Potter and that of the occult. Abanes shows himself to be something of an expert in the history of the occult, but his understanding of how literature works is less helpful.

Francis Bridger, *A Charmed Life: The Spirituality of Potterworld* (London: DLT November 2001). The morality, theology and metaphysics of Potterworld, how these should be assessed and how its the themes may be used as entry points for the gospel in contemporary culture.

Andrew Goddard, 'Harry Potter and the Quest for Virtue' in *Anvil* 18/3. A stimulating article which considers questions of power, education and moral formation in the light of the Harry Potter stories.

John Houghton, *A Closer Look at Harry Potter* (Eastbourne: Kingsway, 2001). A short but illuminating text that considers the effect that the stories have on children, and begins to ask some of the deeper questions.

Margaret Masson, 'The Harry Potter Debate' in *Anvil* 18/3. A helpful article which shows how the concerns some Christians have are based on a narrow understanding of what literature is about. Masson suggests a richer way of reading which highlights the potential, and not the problems, of Harry Potter.

Marc Shapiro, *J K Rowling: The Wizard behind Harry Potter* (London: John Blake, 2000). A light romp through the story of J K Rowling's life so far.